FOR TRENDY LADIES — Taronga Zoo, Sydney

THE DROUGHT BREAKER — Cork Station, Winton, Qld.

DINKY-DI DUNNIES

DOUGLASS BAGLIN / YVONNE AUSTIN

THE DINKUM PRESS

Published by The Dinkum Press
100 Pacific Highway, St Leonards, NSW, Australia 2065
Phone: (02) 437 6311
First published Nov. 1983
© Douglass Baglin and Yvonne Austin 1983
Printed in Singapore by Toppan Printing Co. (S) Pte Ltd.
38 Liu Fang Rd, Jurong, Singapore, 2262

National Library of Australia Cataloguing-in-Publication Data

Baglin, Douglass, 1926.
    Dinky-Di Dunnies.

    ISBN 0 949369 00 4.

    1. Privies – Pictorial works. I. Austin, Yvonne. II. Title.

690

A BUM IN A GUM — Cobar, N.S.W.

— Cockburn, S.A.

HELLO COCKY! — Blaney, N.S.W.

HMV PISSAPHONE — Rocklynne Braford Stud, Orange, N.S.W.

FOR SILLY ASSES — Alpha, Qld.

A REAL PRO

— Great artist Pro Hart,
Broken Hill, N.S.W.

DUNEDOO'S ELECTRIC CHAIR — Dunedoo, N.S.W.

FOR LADY BIRDS ONLY — Mungo National Park, N.S.W.

PRICKLY PEAR — Tomingley, N.S.W.

GENTS WITH SHINGLES — Forbes, N.S.W.

TRANSPLANTS WHILE YOU WAIT — Adelaide

FOR LIBERATED LADIES

— Melbourne

MEN FOR SALE AND LADIES IN WAITING — Sale, Vic.

PARADE, FALL IN! — Cam's Wharf, Lake Macquarie, N.S.W.

FOR MEN WHO NEVER TIRE — Nevertire, N.S.W.

FOR 44 GALLON BUMS — Gidgiealpa Station, via Moonba, S.A.

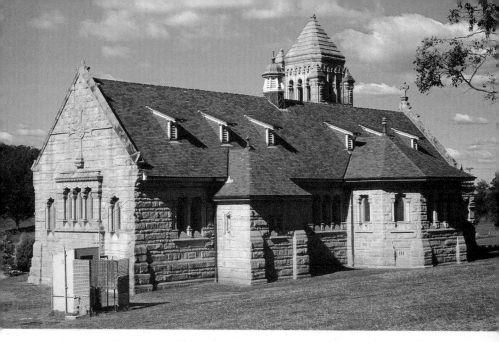

HOLY WATER — The King's School, Parramatta, N.S.W.

HERITAGE DOWN THE DUNNY! — Medical School, Sydney University

THE BLADDER LADDER — Merredin, W.A.

TRICKLE IRRIGATION — Dagworth Station, Winton, Qld.

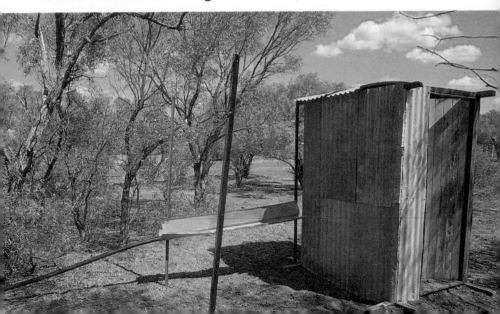

FROM BILLY TEA TO BILLY PEE — Nyngan, N.S.W.

FOR RETIRED IRON KNOBS — Iron Knob, S.A.

HARD PRESSED
— Wollongong, N.S.W.

NO SWEET PEAS — Kingston Cemetery, S.A.

THE WONDER OF WONGARBON — Wongarbon, N.S.W.

HAVE ONE ON ME! — Honour Roll, Beaumaris R.S.L Club, Vic.

FOR LADIES ONLY
— Auburn, S.A.

FOR GUARDS WHO
PULL LEVERS
— Mudgee Railway
Station, N.S.W.

THE BOG — Brunette Downs 2-UP School, N.T.

CONTROL BOX — Adelaide

LAVATREE — Oxley, N.S.W.

A COOLAH LOO AT DUNEDOO — Dunedoo, N.S.W.

THE WEE HOUSE — Wee Waa, N.S.W.

**WIND JAMMER
— Albany, W.A.**

THE BOOBY TRAP — Missions to Seamen, Melbourne

H.M.A.S. LOO LOO — Como, N.S.W.

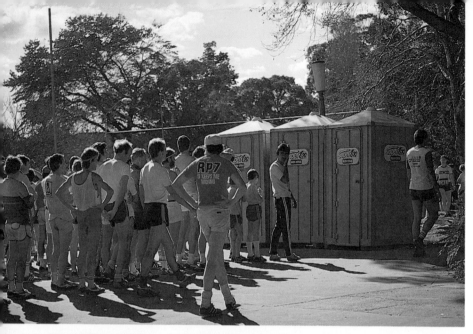

SOME FUN RUN! — Sydney to Surf Run

WIND IN THE WILLOWS — Lowlands, The Serpentine, W.A.

A CAN CAN — White Cliffs, N.S.W.

**BONG BONG
B A N G!!**
— Catholic
Church,
Sale, Vic.

RELIEF CENTRE - GIVE GENEROUSLY — Anglican Cathedral, Brisbane

COCK-A-DODDLE-DOO – Anglican Cathedral, Newcastle, N.S.W.

DON'T FORGET TO PULL THE CHAIN!
— Cordillo Downs Station, via Innamincka, S.A.

WIND PUMP - I'LL HUFF AND I'LL PUFF! — via Dubbo, N.S.W.

PROFESSOR WATERHOUSE'S WATERHOUSE
— Eryldene, Gordon, N.S.W.

FOR EXPRESS PURPOSES — Dubbo, N.S.W.

A BOOZER LOSER — Queensberry Hotel, Melbourne

FOR PUFFING BILLIES — Brisbane

Pssssssssssssss! — Mudgee, N.S.W.

R.I.P. — Adelaide Cemetery

TIME BOMB — Narrabri, N.S.W.

ROCKS AREA — Sydney

BUM CHUMS — Gulgong, N.S.W.

THE THINK TANK — Balladonia Station, Nullabor, W.A.

TRAVELLERS' TALES — Wilcannia, N.S.W.

FOR TOMATO BUMS — Cudgegong, N.S.W.

— Condobolin,
N.S.W.

OH, WHAT A LOVELY STORK — Bellingen, N.S.W.

FOR BABY SITTERS — Mt Poole Station, Milparinka, N.S.W.

DING DONG DELL PUSSY'S ON THE WELL — Quirindi, N.S.W.

AMENITIES BLOCK — Ariah Park, N.S.W.

FOR OUTBACK BUMS
— Cordillo Downs Station, via Innamincka, S.A.

OOPS! — One Tree Hotel, via Hay, N.S.W.

ONE ACRE - DEPOSIT REQUIRED — Back of Bourke, N.S.W.

GEMSTONES FOR SALE — Andamooka, S.A.

FOR GAME COCKS AND CLUCKY HENS

— Under Royal Patronage. In 1924
His Royal Highness The Prince of Wales
and Lord Mountbatten stayed here.

— Canonbar Station, Nyngah, N.S.W.

FOR SQUARE PEGS AND ROUND HOLES — Alice Springs, N.T.

PORTI-POTTI — Pearson's Lookout, N.S.W.

AE & KE Sullivan
OWNER·BUILDER,
Lic. No. 117281
LOT 7
SEC 3

FOR WOOD WORMS AT TUMBLE DOWN DICK
— via Terrey Hills, N.S.W.

BUILDING BOOM! — Cumnock, N.S.W.

DUNNY CAN BAND — The Great Dunny Burn, Tongala, Vic.

FILLING THE DUNNY — The Great Dunny Burn, Tongala, Vic.

CAPTAIN HORNBLOWER — The Great Dunny Burn, Tongala, Vic.

THE LAST POST — The Great Dunny Burn, Tongala, Vic.

A new dinkum Australian festival emerged in October, 1982 when thousands of people flocked to Tongala to celebrate the connection of the sewer and farewell the old dinkum dunnies. For 2 days and nights festivities rang out. The park, exhibiting a fine selection of dinkum dunnies, toilet memorbilia, a dunny can band and children dressed as red back spiders, was the venue for most of the fun. Dunny can lids lined in a row "invited" children to throw toilet rolls through the holes. Men, with dunny cans of water slung over each shoulder, thundered down and over obsticle courses in the Dunny Can Race. Urged on by the crowd's screams of laughter, the Plumbers Handicap provided the spectacle of peculiar arrangements of pipes and fittings. In between the games and races, singers, dancer and comedians entertained. The Royal Australian Naval Band displayed its precision and splendour, and an auction with many dunny products proved amusing. These happy fun-filled days which also sported dinner and concerts culminated in the burning of the dunny. At 6.00 p.m., as the sun was setting, the Royal Australian Naval Band played a tribute before the "dunny" and crowds. In silence the last post was played and the dunny was set ablaze. This happy mischief followed by a dunny dance, raised thousands of dollars for Anti Cancer Research. It is hoped the spirit and usefulness of this Great Dunny Burn may spread to other Australian towns.

GAWD, MOM'S CURRY WAS HOT! — The Great Dunny Burn, Tongala, Vic